A Leaf Falls

Grazia Deledda

Verses, Quotes and Aphorisms

Translated into English by Irma Kurti

Ukiyoto Publishing

All global publishing rights are held by

Ukiyoto Publishing

Published in 2022

Content Copyright © Irma Kurti

ISBN 9789359207513

*All rights reserved.
No part of this publication may be reproduced, transmitted, or stored in a retrieval system, in any form by any means, electronic, mechanical, photocopying, recording or otherwise, without the prior permission of the publisher.*

The moral rights of the author have been asserted.

This is a work of fiction. Names, characters, businesses, places, events, locales, and incidents are either the products of the author's imagination or used in a fictitious manner. Any resemblance to actual persons, living or dead, or actual events is purely coincidental.

This book is sold subject to the condition that it shall not by way of trade or otherwise, be lent, resold, hired out or otherwise circulated, without the publisher's prior consent, in any form of binding or cover other than that in which it is published.

Preface

Grazia Deledda (Nuoro, 27 September 1871–Roma 15 August 1936) was an Italian writer who received the Nobel Prize for Literature in 1926 "for her idealistically inspired writings which with plastic clarity picture the life on her native island and with depth and sympathy deal with human problems in general". She was the first Italian woman to receive the prize, and only the second woman after Selma Lagerlöf was awarded hers in 1909.

Sardinia, a rugged island of ancestral beauty, the archetype of all places, is a timeless land where the dramas told by Grazia Deledda are consummated. And it is in this geographical context that Sardinia takes on the leading role in the writer's literary activity.

All of her works are impregnated with the magical and suspended atmosphere that one breathes here where Deledda saw the light in 1871.

Her literary production is large and intense such as to make her a prolific and complete author.

She starts as a young girl and continues throughout her life, especially as a self-taught woman who was barred from higher education.

Many themes recur in her works—patriarchal ethics of the Sardinian world, the presence of

Fate that governs human existence, prey to superior forces, in which the fragile lives of men are like "reeds in the wind".

These themes are then intertwined with other topics, all equally intense, such as the power of passion, the sense of sin and the need for atonement, in a vaguely religious conception of life. All permeated by an atmosphere full of intense and wild affection.

In particular, the narrative discussion dear to Deledda, and on which she dwells in all her work, is that of real life—strong events of love, pain and death, on which the perception of sin and guilt breathes, as well as that the awareness of the inevitability. Then vigorously emerges the Pietas, understood as compassionate participation in all that is mortal, merciful feelings that lead to forgiveness and rehabilitation by expressing them, Deledda also makes herself a great woman.

Carolina Colombi

Contents

Verses	1
A leaf falls	2
Why?	3
Spring	4
The silent morning Mass	5
My little flower	6
The night	7
Traveling clouds	8
Sunset time	9
Idyll	10
Honeymoon in Sardinia	11
Christmas Eve	12
Miniature	15
In the afternoon	16
The dawn	17
We are Sardinians	18
Quotes And Aphorisms	19
A Short Biography of the Translator	86
About the Author	*88*

Verses
FROM 1887–1900

A Leaf Falls

A leaf falls and it looks as if
it was tint of sun, that in the falling
has the iridescence of a butterfly;
but as soon as it touches the soil
it mingles with the shadow; it's already dead.

Why?

Why does my heart beat fast
when you're next to me and
my eye always turns to you
as the sunflower does the sun?

Why when you go far, my soul
is covered by a black cloak?
Why are you followed assiduously
by the flight of my thought?

Spring

Winter had also cooled the color of the rocks. From the mountains came down silver veins, a thousand silent rivulets, sparkling among the vivid green of the grass. The torrent winced at the bottom of the valley between peach trees and the flowering almond trees. Everything was so pure, young, fresh under the silvery light sky.

The Silent Morning Mass

The temple is silent; pale and diffident,
with the modest dress of the morning,
she came to hear mass with slow steps—
the silent morning mass.

He, who knew it, at the same time
went to the temple and sat close to her,
he never ceases, with ecstatic eyes,
to stare at her sad figurine.

She sees him, but in the vast temple
a mystical perfume of saint reigns,
a sweet pious silence,

that of the aurora in the chaste dawn
her soul pays no attention to her love
but she prays, changes, and thinks only of God.

My Little Flower

It's born and grows in a lawn corner
in the saddest meadow full of frost,
a gentle and delicate flower
with the sweetest colors of the sky:
brother of viola, perfumed,
smiling on her languid stem,
poor flower; hyacinth we call you,
yet over every flower—hyacinth, I love you!

The Night

In the deep night, I watch over the distant
mountains asleep in the lunar dream:
The clear sky is a great sea of innocence
and peace. Oh, vain dreams—

of the dark world, wicked and profane,
where are you? From this
sacred altar, I feel the purest aromas exhale
to the pure stars from the dormient fields,

and to this lonely and radiant peace
the heart graps the high mystery.
When the pure and disdainful soul

sees evil triumphing and the lies,
then it is upset to feel alone like
an eagle, and it dreams curled up.

Traveling Clouds

Autumn comes again, the warm dreaming autumn—
the sky is silver, glaucous silver on the horizon;
sudden water distances in the green plains, pale
open wide to the tender west; wandering purple
clouds pass in pieces like feathers of huge red birds.
Venus sets. Everything is mystery in this enigmatic
season; the glaucous evening, the faint smell
of chrysanthemums; the wandering red clouds,
the tremulous illusion of the waters and of the green
plains to the west; the tender, occult thought donated
to a distant heart that I ruined for us in desperate love;
a thought that the traveling red clouds accompany;
and never, like them, reaches its fate.

Sunset Time

The dead sky is purple: pale vapors
from the gray mountains exhale,
and sadly, on the slopes the fires
of the subsoilers shine far away.

Red leaves fall and, in the twilight,
seem to be circling a flowers'shower.
The last dying crickets are groaning
a ballad of painful loves.

It is an hour of universal sadness:
with the light every joy seems over;
and the memory that you lied to me.

The soul that seemed so ideal
vapors bitterly that lethal fog, which
now obscures all the infinity.

Idyll

I am pale and dark. A proud love
reveals my dark sad pupil,
cold hands, white dress,
tall and thin, always a light step.

I am of burning Saracen blood,
and he is of noble Latin blood.
In his eyes laugh the opal, sweet
reflection of the seas of the East.

We live only on dreams, and although
laughter never brightens up our pale
semblants, we run a life of paradise—
him and me, two fervent lovers.

Honeymoon in Sardinia

The newlyweds ride on a black filly:
he has the gun, she in red costume
looks like a pomegranate flower;
high around the corn sways like
a sea, a poplar stirred by the breeze
flickers silvery in the silvery evening.

They come back from the party—altered.
She remembers the circle of native dances
where she reigned. He won at the target.
Their front appears to be surrounded
of diadems of dreams and hopes.
And the black filly trots and trots...

Christmas Eve

The sad evening falls behind the humid
profiles of the desolate hills,
a waxy melancholy lace smokes
of cold fog.

In the painful fields, where yesterday
the treacherous hurricane passed
devastating, looms high the silence
of things—dead and defeated.

How much sadness inside the snowy skies,
where the fog fades like a dream;
how cold in the poet's thought,
and in his heart!

Across the gray glass up the slender
naked copper of the silent landscape,
the thought wanders and asks—ah,
in so much desolation,

in the gloomy night that this cold
vesper foretells, will you come down
Christian dawn of splendor and joy,
Baby Jesus?

If you come down, I'll stay up here in
the freezing cold space of my balcony
waiting for you, and when bright you
will pass before me,

I'll tell you with extended pleading hands:
for this year, Jesus, this year come down,
in the dark and desolate huts
and in the sheepfolds

of the shepherds who first sang to you
the hosanna; come down and look; you know
that yesterday's hurricane also dispersed
their flocks.

Miniature

The vermilion sunset,
a fire in the west.
Against this fiery
background rises only
one green branch of
cherry tree and the new
moon among the shining
sparse foliage: nothing,
nothing else but a brunette
head on the green branch
leans and her bright gaze
dreams and gets lost
in the vermilion dusk.

In the Afternoon

Sweet dreams, like honey, offers
the warm afternoon: on the opal
of the sweetest sky, at the siesta,
in vague dreams, the spirit rises,

and in the blue immensity, it stops—
lulled by the strange and musical
voice of a distant, high and yellow
forest, smiled by the autumn sun.

Wakefulness or sleep? Every thought
is mild, all is persuasive sweetness,
delicate and fine voluptuousness;

the desire for the unknown, infinite
ecstasy closes its eyes softly
as for the sleep of eternity.

The Dawn

How sweet it is to wake up in the morning
close to you! If already so much sweetness
it is to think, upon waking up, of a loved
one far away, what an immense joy this is
to return from the kingdom of oblivion
and see the light again within two good
adored eyes and tighten everything in
my hands with your beloved head, all
the dream of our life. And the dawn in
golden circles shine behind the glass,
girding like some enchanted rings
the nest of our immense and pure love.

We are Sardinians

We are Sardinians.

We are Spaniards, Africans, Phoenicians, Carthaginians,

Romans, Arabs, Pisans, Byzantines, Piedmontese.

We are the golden yellow gorses that fall

on the rocky paths like great lighted lamps.

We are the wild solitude, the immense and profound silence,

the splendor of the sky, the white flower of the cistus.

We are the unbroken reign of the mastic tree,

of the waves that flow from the ancient granites,

of the dog rose,

of the wind, of the immensity of the sea.

We are an ancient land of long silences,

of gloomy plants, of wide and pure horizons,

of mountains burned by the sun and vengeance.

We are Sardinians.

Quotes And Aphorisms

*****

I was born in Sardinia. My family, made up of wise but also violent people and primitive artists, had authority and even a library. But when I started writing at thirteen, I was contradicted by my parents. The philosopher warns: if your son writes verses, correct him and send him to the mountain road; if you find him engaged with the poem the second time, punish him again; if he goes for the third time, leave him alone because he is a poet. Without vanity, it happened to me like this too. I had an irresistible mirage of the world, especially of Rome. And in Rome, after the splendor of my youth, I built my house where I live quietly with my partner, listening to the ardent words of my young children.

I have had all the things a woman can ask of her destiny, but greater above all luck, faith in life and God. I lived with the winds, with the woods, with the mountains. For days, months and years I watched the slow unfolding of the clouds in the Sardinian sky. I have placed my head a thousand and a thousand times on the trunks of trees, on the stones, on the rocks to listen to the voice of the leaves, what the birds said, what the running water told. I saw the sunrise and sunset, the rising of the moon in the immense solitude of the mountains, I listened to the songs, traditional music and fairy tales and speeches of the people. And so my art was formed, like a song, or a motif that springs spontaneously from the lips of a primitive poet.

(Grazia Deledda, from her speech on the occasion of the delivery of the Nobel Prize)

*****

*****

If your child wants to be a writer or poet, strongly advise against it. If he continues, threaten him to disinherit him. Beyond these tests, if he resists, you begin to thank God for giving you an inspired son, different from the others.

*****

We all change, from one day to the next, through slow and unconscious evolutions, conquered by that ineluctable law of time which today finishes erasing what yesterday had written in the mysterious boards of the human heart.

*****

*****

Is it possible that we cannot live without hurting the innocent?

*****

We are all a mixture of good and evil, but the latter must be overcome, Antonio. The steel that is steel is tempered and reduced to a sword by those who want to defeat the enemy.

*****

*****

Life passes and we let it pass like river water, and only when it is lacking do we realize that it is lacking.

*****

Love is what binds man to woman, and money is what binds woman to man.

*****

*****

A free man is always suitable for a free woman. It is enough to exist love.

*****

Like children and the elderly, she began to cry without knowing why, of pain that was joy, of joy that was pain.

*****

*****

"We have to adapt," Efix said, pouring him a drink. "Look at the water: why do they say it is wise? Because it takes the shape of the vase where it is poured."

"Even the wine, I think!"

"Even the wine, yes! Except that the wine sometimes foams and runs away; but the water, no."

"Even the water, if it's put on the fire to boil," Natòlia said.

*****

"And why be born?"

"Oh beautiful, because God wills it so!"

*****

*****

"And my mistresses? Don't they notice?"

"They? They are like the wooden saints in churches. They look, but they do not see. Evil does not exist for them."

*****

"The remedy is in us," affirmed the old woman. "Heart, you must have, nothing else..."

*****

*****

Efix ate and told, with uncertain words, veiled with timid lies; but when he had thrown the crumbs and the bottom of the glass on the floor since the earth always wants its little part of man's nourishment, he straightened up a little on his back and his eyes circled with radiant lines.

*****

"We were born to suffer like Him; we must cry and be silent..." he whispered. And this was his wish.

*****

*****

Donna Ester, remembering that he liked flowers, plucked a geranium from the well and placed it between his fingers on the crucifix. Finally, she covered the corpse with a green silk carpet that they had pulled out for the wedding. But the carpet was short, and his feet remained uncovered, facing the door as usual; and it seemed that the servant slept one last time in the noble house resting before embarking on the journey toward eternity.

*****

*****

After a week of furious wind, sleet and rain, the tops of the mountains appeared white among the black clouds that lowered and disappeared on the horizon and the village of Oronou with its reddish houses built on the gray summit of a granite peak, with its steep and rocky paths, seemed to emerge from the fog as if it had escaped the flood.

At his feet, the torrents thundered down noisily in the valley, and in the distance, in the plains and countryside of Siniscola, the swamps and overflowing rivers sparkled in the rays of the sun rising from the sea. The whole landscape, from the mountains to the coast, from the dark line of the plateau above Oronou to the thickets at the bottom of the valley, seemed to be dripping water.

*****

*****

The house was simple but comfortable—two large rooms per floor, a little low, with wooden floors and ceilings whitewashed with lime; the entrance divided in the middle by a wall—on the right the staircase, the first flight of granite steps, the rest of slate; on the left some steps leading down to the cellar. The solid door, fastened with a large iron hook, had a knocker that knocked like a hammer, and a bolt and lock with a key the size of a castle. The room to the left of the entrance was used for many things, with a high hard bed, a desk, a large walnut wardrobe, chairs almost rustic, stuffed, and cheerfully painted blue. The one on the right was the dining room, with a chestnut table, chairs like the others, and a fireplace with a beaten floor. Nothing else. A solid door too, secured by hooks and bolts, led into the kitchen. The kitchen was, as in all still patriarchal houses, the most inhabited environment, the most tepid of life and intimacy.

*****

*****

We are in Sardinia, in the mountainous part of Sardinia, in a small town that we will content ourselves with calling only X, although on the map it is marked with a very loud and long name. X owns its good promenade, its squares, still free of marble fountains and statues, its splendid cafes, its "club", and sometimes even at intervals of two or three years, it allows itself the luxury of the theater. However, all this does not prevent anyone from living the most boring life of this world, so that the smallest novelty is enough to stir the peaceful inhabitants with little interest in the serious questions of distant mountains and seas.

*****

*****

Goulliau and his wife went down the Nazionale Street. It was early November, but it was already cold and the air was still humid and foggy under the overcast sky.

At that hour, between eight and nine, Nazionale Street was almost deserted between two smoky backgrounds, under the purple light, now alive, now dull, of the electric lamps; many shops were already closed, the sidewalks seemed wider than usual; the trams rushed down, moaning, amidst a fantastic splendor of violet sparks that appeared and disappeared on the damp tracks. In the distant desert of Termini square, the jet of the fountain shot through the fog like an enormous stem of lilac-colored crystal.

*****

*****

To escape, or at least attempt to escape from an unhappiness that fate had sent her for free, the young woman got herself another one at the price of six thousand lire.

Six thousand lire for two months of renting a villa in a luxury health resort is not much. The trouble is that the health resort was three kilometers away, and the villa was reduced to a nice little house outside with its good tower crenellated and the marble loggia, and inside a hovel without light, without water, with the owl's nest on the terrace, the walls splashed with dead mosquitoes and a furnace temperature.

*****

*****

Despite all the necessary precautions and measures, our honeymoon was disastrous. We got married in May and left soon after. Roses, roses, roses accompanied us—the girls threw them from their windows, with handfuls of wheat and glances of loving envy. The station was all garlanded with them, and the hedges of the valley were also reddish. Roses and wheat—love and luck, everything smiled at us. The destination of our journey was safe, suitable for the occasion—a small house between the countryside and the sea, where my husband had already spent some time before. An elderly woman, discreet, good at housework, already known to him, would take care of all our material needs.

*****

*****

It was one evening last April that the landowner Davide D'Elia, returning from a gig from one of his farms, thought he saw a lost lamb in the middle of the road. Looking closer he realized that it was a child, wrapped in an old scarf of black fur; so small that when the vehicle arrived it did not even move, so much that the horse itself, not having time to dodge, stopped abruptly.

*****

*****

Maria Concezione left the small hospital of her town on December 7th, the eve of her name day. She had undergone a serious operation; her left breast had been completely removed, and, in dismissing her, the head physician had told her with Olympic and crystalline cruelty:

"You are lucky enough not to be very young anymore. You are twenty-eight, I think. Evil will take a long time to reproduce—ten, even twelve years. In any case, be very respectful. Do not overwork, do not look for emotions. Tranquility, eh? And let yourself be seen sometimes."

*****

*****

Even that night Paulo was preparing to go out.

His mother, in her room adjoining his, could hear him move stealthily. Perhaps he was waiting for her to switch off the light and go to bed to get out.

She put out the light but did not go to bed. Sitting by her door, she clutched her hard servant's hands, still wet from the rinsing of the dishes, pressing her thumbs over each other to gain strength. But from that moment, the uneasiness in her grew. It overcame her obstinacy in hoping that her son would calm down, that, as in the past, he would read or go to sleep. For a few minutes, the young priest's furtive footsteps ceased. Outside the sound of the wind accompanied by the murmur of the trees of the ridge behind the small parish could be heard. Wind not too strong but incessant and monotonous that enveloped the house with a great strident ribbon, tighter and tighter, and attempted to uproot it from its foundations and pull it down.

*****

*****

At twenty-five, beautiful, rich, engaged, without ever having felt great pain, one day Maria Magda suddenly felt her heart black and empty.

It was like the beginning of a physical illness, which increased day by day— spreading across her whole being.

She was happy in her house and another kind of happiness awaited her. But to reach the new happiness, she had to abandon the old one. And it seemed to her that then the regret of the distant family, of the sweet paternal home, of the lost freedom, of the abandoned homeland, would give her an unspeakable nostalgia, poisoning her new happiness.

*****

*****

One night, last December, I stayed for more than two hours listening carefully to a woman from Orosei who told me the legends of the castle of Galtellì.

Her accent was so sincere and her conviction so ingrained that I often stared at her with an indefinable gasp, wondering if, by chance, these bizarre supernatural stories, which run through the people's farmhouses, have a foundation and something true.

*****

*****

The saints, Our Lady and Jesus himself often take part in many Sardinian legends. There is no Madonna that does not have her history, and almost all the churches, especially the country churches—the small brown churches lost in the desolate plains or in the lonely mountains that bear the imprint of Pisan or Andalusian buildings—are surrounded by a simple or legendary tradition.

*****

*****

A palm tree whose leaves looked like blades of swords rusted by the sea wind, stood between the last house of the village and the moor that ended in the sea.

The village seemed uninhabited, and to add to this impression there were a few ruins here and there covered in yellowish moss and populated with lizards. Even the walls of the little house with the palm tree and those of the courtyard that flanked it, crumbled and flattened; and around the windows, with their discolored shutters, the reddish stones could be seen.

*****

*****

It may seem like a novel to you, my blonde and little reader, but it is a true story—so true that I, to tell you about it, change the names of the people and places to whom and where it happened.

Let's imagine that we are in Sardinia, in my green and unknown Sardinia, and let's start.

*****

*****

It's an August morning. Over the wide sky, enclosed by the thin and jagged lines of the mountains, turned blue by the distance, large ashy clouds pass like flocks of fog, which vanish on the still limpid strips of blue.

*****

*****

Childhood! Is it perhaps a magical and mysterious word, an oriental hieroglyph, understood indiscriminately by the soul, by the mind, by the heart, where it awakens sweet, very sweet memories, although faded in the mists of the past and smiles wandering and sweet like those memories and gasps of regret and forgetfulness of the present?

*****

*****

In R...my little hometown we arrived around eight. It is impossible to describe the strange impression I felt when I saw my countryside, my valley, and my sky again after so many years away.

*****

*****

Uncle Salvatore, our old farmer, began:

"My children, I have not always been a farmer. I was born to become something great, at least a priest, but the circumstances and the extreme poverty of my good mother did not allow it."

*****

*****

Up above, against the azure background of the limestone mountains, under the fresh sky of a deep Flemish landscape sweetness that reminds me of Van-Haanen's best-known paintings, our greenhouse dominated the village. With its roof sharp on the elegant white cornice, the gothic windows on the second floor and the balcony that surrounded it all on the first, slender, high, the green tint glazed by the sun, it looked like a small Chinese house made of porcelain, so fresh and cheerful that still, despite the sad case that I will tell you about that forced me to leave forever, its memory puts a cheerful note in the remembrances of my childhood.

*****

*****

Even in his soul, a vague light reigned, which at times was extinguished completely; and before him stretched out, interminable and mysterious as in a dream, the path of evil.

*****

The marriage of love is the marriage of God; the marriage of convenience is the marriage of the devil.

*****

*****

Stay on the edge of the sea, and count and count all the grains of the earth—when you have counted them all, you will know that they are nothing compared to the years of eternity.

*****

The light wind that rustled in the distant woods seemed to him a confused voice, now sweet, now fearful. What was it saying? What did the wind say? What was the forest murmuring? He would have liked to hear that voice distinct and was anguished, moved, irritated, at not being able to.

*****

*****

The greatest things are said in silence. Look at the moon.

*****

Only the leaves of the reeds moved above the ridge, stiff straight like swords that rolled on the metal of the sky.

"But why this, Efix, tell me, you who have traveled the world. Is it everywhere like this? Why does fate crush us like this, like reeds?"

"Yes," he said then, "we are just like reeds in the wind, my woman Esther. That's why! We are reeds and the fate is the wind."

"Yes, okay, but why this fate?"

"And the wind, why? God only knows."

*****

*****

He felt her lips wet with tears imprint on his fingers like the imprint of a flower wet with dew.

*****

Ah, that's why I don't even like to go back there; it seems to me that I have left something and that I would never find it again…

*****

*****

The recomposed family? The broken vase reattached with mastic, unable to contain the liquid anymore—only air.

*****

Her heart was beating inside her as if it had spread its wings and yearned to fly away.

*****

*****

After all, everyone in life is like this, in prison, to pay the very fault of being alive.

*****

Her thoughts withdraw into their most secret hiding place. No one in the world must know them, and this not so much out of pride as because she loves her soul as her home, that everything is in order, clean, locked up in the coffers, belonging to her alone.

*****

*****

It must have been nice on winter evenings to lie down on the mats in front of the log fire and listen to the voice of the forest in wild conversations with the wind.

*****

I could hear her footsteps behind me like a child's; it reached me and touched me lightly with its muzzle to warn me that it was there as if to ask permission to accompany me. I turned and stroked its velvet head. I immediately felt that I too had a friend in the world.

*****

*****

There are many women who live in the memory of a fantastic love and true love is for them a great and elusive mystery like divinity.

*****

All night it snowed, and the world, like a great ship leaking, seemed to be submerged slowly in this white sea. It seemed to us that we were inside the great ship. We went down, in bad dreams, buried little by little, full of fear but also lulled by hope in God. And the next morning, the good Lord shone a wonderful winter sun on the white earth, where the poplar trunks really looked like the masts of a ship decorated in white.

*****

*****

The August morning was very pure. The day before it had rained, and a sweet coolness reigned in the woods—the ferns, the grass, the trunks, and the washed rocks exhaled an almost irritating scent; the breeze gave silver tides to the foliage of the holm oaks; the sky smiled as blue as a lake in the serene background.

*****

"I am very small" and "bold as a giant".

*****

*****

In the bright streets, in the tall houses beaten by the sun, the wind and the reflection of the sea, everything was light, joy, and poetry.

*****

It seemed to him that all his affections returned, stacked up on his heart, were rotting like fruits that no one had wanted to reap.

*****

*****

The clouds of May passed white and tender as the veils of a woman.

*****

The moon was setting languidly like a half-closed eye on voluptuousness.

*****

*****

Friendship that covers love like the robe a naked body.

*****

The memories covered him thick, alive as the stars that seemed to cover his face.

*****

*****

From a black wall, a blue window as empty as the eye of the past looks at the melancholy pink panorama of the rising sun.

*****

Eagles you have to be; not thrushes.

*****

*****

Large, low, undulating, uniform valleys chase each other as far as the eye can see, speckled with shade, wild and deserted. Not a cottage, a tree, a flock, a street.

*****

The sun was setting behind the river, among shattered metal and pieces of purple like a defeated king.

*****

*****

A nightingale sang on the lonely tree still suffused with smoke. All the coolness of the evening, all the harmony of serene distances, and the smile of the stars to the flowers and the smile of the flowers to the stars, and the proud joy of the beautiful young shepherds and the closed passion of the women in red corsets, and all the melancholy of the poor who live waiting for what was left of the table of the rich, and the distant pains and hopes beyond, and the past, the lost homeland, love, crime, remorse, prayer, the song of the pilgrim who goes and does not know where the night will be but feels guided by God, and the green solitude of the little farm there, the voice of the river and the alders there, the smell of euphorbias, the laughter and weeping of Grixenda, and Noemi's tears and laughter, the laughter and tears of Efix, the laughter and tears of the whole world, trembled and vibrated in the notes of the nightingale above the lonely tree that seemed higher than the mountains, with the top close to the sky and the tip of the last leaf stuck inside a star.

*****

*****

I want to remember the Sardinia of my childhood, but above all, the profound and authentic wisdom, the almost religious way of thinking and living of some old Sardinian shepherds and peasants (...) despite their absolute lack of culture, leads us to believe an atavistic habit of thought and superior contemplation of life and things beyond life. From some of these old men, I have learned truths and knowledge that no book has revealed to me clearer and more consoling. These are the great fundamental truths that the first inhabitants of the earth had to excavate by themselves, teachers and pupils at the same time, in the presence of the great arcana of nature and the human heart...

*****

A Short Biography of the Translator

Irma Kurti is an Albanian poetess, writer, lyricist, journalist, and translator. She is a naturalized Italian. She has been writing since she was a child. In 1980, she was honored with the first national prize on the 35th anniversary of the *Pionieri* magazine for her poem "To my homeland". In 1989, she won the second prize in the National Competition organized by Radio Tirana on the 45th anniversary of the Liberation of Albania.

All her books are dedicated to the memory of her beloved parents Hasan Kurti and Sherife Mezini, who supported and encouraged every step of her literary path.

Kurti has won numerous literary prizes and awards in Italy and Italian Switzerland. She was awarded the "Universum Donna" International Prize IX Edition 2013 for Literature and the lifetime nomination of "Ambassador of Peace" by the University of Peace of Italian Switzerland. In 2020, she received the title of Honorary President of WikiPoesia, the Encyclopedia of Poetry.

In 2021, she was awarded the title "Liria" (Freedom) by the Arbëreshë Community in Italy.

Irma Kurti has published 25 books in Albanian, 17 in Italian and 7 in English. She has written about 150 lyrics for adults and children. She is also the translator of 10 books of different authors and of all her books in Italian and English. She lives in Bergamo, Italy.

About the Author

Irma Kurti

Irma Kurti is an Albanian poetess, writer, lyricist, journalist, and translator. She is a naturalized Italian. She has been writing since she was a child.

Kurti has won numerous literary prizes and awards in Italy and Italian Switzerland. She was awarded the "Universum Donna" International Prize IX Edition 2013 for Literature and the lifetime nomination of "Ambassador of Peace" by the University of Peace of Italian Switzerland. In 2020, she received the title of Honorary President of WikiPoesia, the Encyclopedia of Poetry.

Irma Kurti has published 25 books in Albanian, 17 in Italian and 7 in English. She is also the translator of 10 books of different authors and of all her books in Italian and English. She lives in Bergamo, Italy.

www.ingramcontent.com/pod-product-compliance
Lightning Source LLC
LaVergne TN
LVHW041537070526
838199LV00046B/1713